Find premium content and
innovation resources at

InnovationSteps.com/book

Innovation Step-by-Step: How to Create & Develop Ideas for your Challenge

www.InnovationSteps.com

Editing and cover design by John Praw Kruse. Some images courtesy Depositphotos.com, used with permission.

ISBN-13 978-1499287479
ISBN-10 149928747X

Table of Contents

Introduction

Innovation is a process of change. You can design something new and different that has a real impact when brought to life. Your new innovation could be for a product, service, message, method, or new and better way of doing something. You are innovating when you are working on a challenge by developing and launching a new idea for a desired outcome. I want to help you do this innovation for your own challenge and will show you examples each step along the way.

People are constantly being asked to innovate, and companies declare how much their organizations value innovation. But do all of the people within these organizations *really* understand the steps necessary to develop new ideas into innovations that have a fighting chance at being successful?

If you find yourself in a situation looking to innovate, this book can help you do just that. You will learn the steps of a widely-applicable innovation system and the key activities to make your innovation vision a reality. Furthermore, you will get to look over my shoulder as I do my own innovation project.

My innovation project was developing a new product, a resource that would help people learn innovation, and the result was this book! After learning about each step, you can do the same activities I did, using my examples, to build your own portfolio of innovative concepts. You can communicate and launch new ideas of your own by using this guide and our InnovationSteps.com program.

How to Use This Book

Are you being asked to do more with less? Do you need to build and launch new initiatives, products, or services? Do you need to communicate or market more effectively or develop your business? Do you need to make money, save money, or save time? Do you need to contribute to a culture of innovation in your organization? You can work on any of these challenges with a systematic approach to develop solutions.

Innovation begins with an important challenge or problem. Innovation is more than just creativity or idea generation. It includes development of the ideas you generate, further refinement, and implementation of the idea with a goal of solving the problem or responding to your challenge with something of value.

As you move through this book, you will follow a process to build your own portfolio of innovative concepts that you too can develop, communicate and launch!

Innovation is helpful for individuals who want to:
- Do much more with much less
- Succeed sooner and have more options
- Be more creative and effective in work and life
- Make rapid progress on a challenge
- Solve problems and seize opportunities

Organizations use innovation to:
- Develop new products
- Offer new services
- Generate new sources of revenue
- Save money or reduce expenses
- Develop a more positive culture
- Collaborate, learn, and develop

You or your organization could work on any of the general challenges above, or you can create your own more specific challenge for innovation. The challenge you choose could be entrepreneurial, personal, or have an organizational focus.

Why Innovate?

Responding Naturally to Change

In many cases, we need to innovate because we must respond to some kind of change. This change could be something we perceive as negative and want to fix. It could be something we know is beneficial, so we need to seize the opportunity. Or we could be uncertain as to the ramifications of the change. In any case, change is natural, and responding to it with growth and innovation should be natural too.

One thing we don't want to do is stay the same, not respond to change, and wither. Refuse to change, and you might find yourself less relevant or useful, like those unused, old cassette tapes collecting dust in your attic.

Doing nothing when innovation is needed is often the worst option. As we know, change is always happening, making innovation important on a continual basis. Change is only happening faster. Without innovation, you can become out of date and left behind like an old typewriter or tube TV on the curb.

The Frog Metaphor

There is a great metaphor that relates to our need to respond to change. Let's think about why we need to take action to change by looking at the frog. Frogs like water. This frog is in a pot of water at room temperature. In this pot, the frog is comfortable, so he'll hang out there. But if we take the frog out and put him into a pot of water that's boiling, it's a shock. The frog will jump out of there right away!

Now, let's put the frog back into a pot that's at room temperature, where the frog is comfortable. If we turn on the burner to slowly heat the water, slowly but surely bringing it to a boil, what happens?

Sooner rather than later, the frog becomes frog

soup. He never saw the clear-cut need to jump out of the pot. He never had a direct signal to change, and it crept up on him gradually. The moral of the story is…don't get too comfortable. Change and jump before it gets too hot!

Root Down and Branch Out

This is why we need to always be innovating. We may not always get thrown into a pot of boiling water and need to jump or respond, but I think many of us can feel the heat as it creeps up. In this case it is better to react sooner rather than later.

We need to always be thinking innovation through rooting down and branching out in our lives. We take action to grow and develop new strategies for what we can do next from our strong foundation (our roots) of our expertise and what is working well. We branch out and try new things that are rooted in what we do best and take action by thoughtfully generating new ideas and responding to change.

Don't conduct the frog experiment at home, but do conduct the oak tree experiment: grow and change through the seasons by rooting down and branching out.

Innovation is a powerful thing. It is also a natural thing. Like the oak tree, we are designed to grow and change.

Visualize Your Innovation Future

Innovation Inspires Motivation!

Innovation is a motivator to take action. If you are like me, you enjoy that moment of creativity - to come up with that new idea. We love to figure out how to do something better, or solve a problem. We love to take these opportunities and make something positive happen.

What kind of future do you want to realize? What is your innovation vision? In this activity, you will visualize a very positive image of your future. This will help you begin to think about your innovation project.

Dream It and See It in Your Mind

Pretend it is one year from now, and imagine you have launched a successful innovation. You spent the time to develop some ideas, turn them into concepts, and launch them.

What was the result of all that work? What do you see in your mind?

What happened? What does the future look like now? What is your work like? What is your group like? What is your organization like?

In what areas have things become better or different?

Pretend we are meeting one year from now. Visualize yourself reporting on how excellent the last year has been. What is your innovation vision, and what is the result you imagine?

Write down or sketch out your vision. Think of it like a YouTube highlight video. What would be in that video? Draw it out. Capture the dream your mind is giving you. This is your vision of an innovation future.

The Innovation System

To successfully innovate and develop our ideas to impact, we need to approach innovation systematically, moving through steps or stages.

The innovation step-by-step system has been developed and refined over the years thanks to many sources of experience. I've led innovation projects with a wide variety of organizations and institutions. I've designed and facilitated hundreds of workshops and programs. I've hosted numerous brainstorming sessions and collected data on each of them. I've also researched and read the literature as well as attended conferences and events. Through these avenues I test out the activities of this system and even launch my own innovations using these tools. Through all of these sources I've synthesized an innovation system that helps you systematically develop ideas for your challenge and see your innovations come to life.

Starting new things is not always easy. New things fail all the time, so we need to increase our likelihood for success. A best-practice and systematic approach can help us succeed sooner.

How to Innovate: 7 Steps to Developing Innovative Ideas

This innovation system is a process we go through step-by-step, and activity-by-activity. These are the seven steps you will follow throughout the course of this guide.

This overview will help you anticipate what is to come, but don't worry about memorizing or learning the steps now. We'll delve deeper into each step as we come to it.

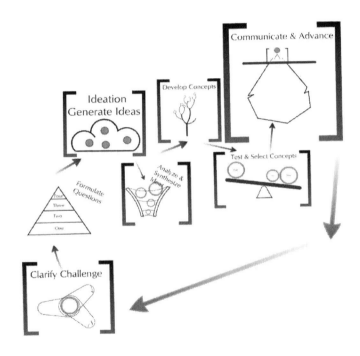

1. **Clarify the challenge.** Research to identify problems and opportunities. Start with a meaningful challenge, and gain insight. Get the opinion of the people you serve. What

do they think the problems, challenges, and opportunities are? We need a diversity of views to get a clear idea of what the challenge really is. You probably know what many of these people think, and you may know how to get more specific insight from them.

2. **Formulate questions.** Break that challenge down. Turn it into a series of questions, and organize those questions from the most general to the most specific. A large number of general questions will lead to more focused and specific questions.

3. **Generate ideas.** Use those questions to generate ideas. Gather a lot of ideas. Generate them yourself, and gather them from outside sources. Observe what ideas arise, but don't judge them yet! Go for quantity and diversity of ideas.

4. **Analyze and synthesize ideas.** Sort these ideas out once you have a lot of them. Throw them into a funnel to narrow them down. Sift and winnow. Go from many ideas to the ones you want to really develop. See what themes naturally emerge in your idea list.

5. **Develop concepts.** Flesh out your ideas a

bit more. Build and extend them. Develop the best ideas into full-blown concepts.

6. **Test and select concepts.** You're getting close to launching your innovation. Test out the concepts that remain to see if some are better than others. See how your stakeholders feel about these concepts. Validate them.

7. **Communicate and advance.** Communicate to others your top concept. This helps you gain valuable feedback to improve both your concept and your skill at communicating it. You can always improve your concept, but now you are ready to take action and launch your concept. Get it out into the world! Remember, you went through each stage of the innovation process for the purpose of launching your idea. You should not feel like it has to be perfect before you go public with it.

Innovation never stops, so keep working on it. Activate your idea and keep working through the innovation process to keep making it better. Start over again with the open loop of innovation. The best way to innovate successfully is to make active and continuous innovation a part of your culture.

Your Innovation Project Space

We will soon get started guiding you through the innovation system. It is important to capture and store all of these ideas in one place.

Keep in mind that great innovations are not achieved through solitary work. They are the result of collaborations. Involve others to help you generate ideas, develop the concept, validate the concept, and communicate the concept so that it is meaningful and memorable.

You can use collaborative online tools like Google Drive (previously called Google Docs) to involve others, pose your question, provide background, show visuals in the form of a photo or video, and generate ideas. I like to use free tools like Google Drive and Dropbox for my own personal innovation projects, as well as those that I want to show or involve others in. This is an easy way to involve collaborators in your innovation system.

You can also do this with basic tools like Microsoft Word, or even a sheet of paper. Just be sure to capture what you are doing! It is important to get it out of your mind and stored somewhere where you can revisit it and share with others.

Step 1: Clarify the Challenge

Clarify Challenge

An important start to your innovation project is to crystallize the problems and challenges that you intend to solve with new ideas. You must also pose important questions that are grounded in that problem or opportunity for innovation.

One example of an innovation framework that we'll reference in this guide is Google's Project 10^100. In 2008, Google launched a campaign that solicited concept ideas to change the world. They opened a simple question up to the world: What would help the most?

Google then offered seven suggested categories and questions:

1. **Community:** How can we help connect

people, build communities, and protect unique cultures?

2. **Opportunity:** How can we help people better provide for themselves and their families?

3. **Energy:** How can we help move the world toward safe, clean, inexpensive energy?

4. **Environment:** How can we help promote a cleaner and more sustainable global ecosystem?

5. **Health:** How can we help individuals lead longer, healthier lives?

6. **Education:** How can we help more people get more access to better education?

7. **Shelter:** How can we help ensure that everyone has a safe place to live?

These categories were selected because they offer real problems and opportunities. These are starting points. If your vision is to "change the world," then the seven Google categories and questions may be beneficial starting places for you. It is like your own "space" for innovation.

Odds are your own specific challenge may be different, though. Google's categories are also very broad, and you will likely have a more specific challenge that you are addressing. Your challenge will likely be related to the problems or opportunities that exist for you or your organization - specific to your mission.

As you pick your category or understand your space for innovation, think about your expertise, unique strengths, skills, passions, and any other assets you can leverage. Is there a market or interest for your potential innovations in that category? Are there resources and people to draw from within that category that will care about your specific challenge? If so, you are in the right space toward making innovation happen!

Action 1: What is your specific challenge?

Darin's Challenge Example:

I visualized a future where thousands of people could be engaged in working on their own innovation projects with my help - digitally. They are learning and doing innovation for their own challenge with my products or services.

I can turn my challenge into a "BIG Challenge Question" that I can use in the next step.

Mine is: What kinds of affordable products, services, or programs could I develop and launch to help thousands of people learn and do innovation step-by-step by working on their own projects?

Step 2: Formulate Questions

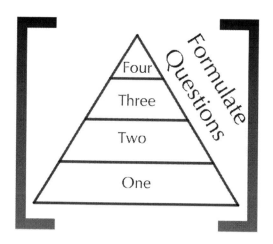

From the first step, you should now have a challenge in mind formulated by problems and opportunities. Generating ideas and innovation from this challenge will help create a more positive future. You may have even naturally thought of some big brainstorming questions related to this challenge already.

Now we want to do some research to make sure that we are moving in the right direction. We want to make sure we are working on the right things. Is there anything missing or something we haven't thought of? What direction should we move in? How do we gain quick insight and validation to decide which questions we'll use to generate ideas?

In order to answer these questions, creating a short survey can provide a great deal of insight. The survey can provide both "write-in" ideas as well as selected answers. The answers help to validate the direction you are moving in, and the write-in ideas may shed light on any blind spots in your innovation vision.

Gathering a dozen responses to a short survey of no more than five questions, which can be done in a couple of minutes, can help you zero in on your direction for innovation before you invest development time later.

Free online tools like Google Drive and Survey Monkey provide effective ways to conduct quick, short surveys to gather insights and validate your current path. They also allow your colleagues or customers to co-create with you in an engaging and interactive format.

To provide a real example, I created online innovation webinars. I'm always seeking to create new webinars that match my expertise and clients' needs. The first webinar series I did (found at InnovationTraining.org) was created based on feedback and insights from clients regarding the topics they wanted to learn more about. Looking for new insights to determine what to create next, I created a short survey.

See for yourself the short online survey example of a tool for innovation you can use for free:

surveymonkey.com/s/MTJJPHN

Leadership Professional Short Survey   Exit this survey

This short qualitative survey for university leaders is about the future goals and challenges that you, your department, and your institution face. Your responses will be anonymous and the results will inform articles and programs for higher education professionals.

1. (You) What are the biggest challenges you face as a higher education professional and leader in the university setting?

The key is to keep it simple. You are looking for new ideas and a direction to move in. A simple survey can do this. Before generating ideas, try to ask people in your network to clarify the challenge that they want solved. In addition to emailing a group, you can collect short survey responses through Twitter, Facebook, your blog, and other social media avenues.

Action 2: Create your own short survey to zero in on your direction for innovation. Gather insight from your stakeholders using Survey Monkey or another online source.

Based on this insight, finalize questions and prepare for the idea generation stage. Based on your validated problems or opportunities, write down a series of questions you would like ideas for.

Darin's Challenge Example:

Based on the insight I got from others on my challenge, I created these more specific questions that I wanted to get feedback on. They helped guide me in very specific directions.

BIG Challenge Question:

1. What kinds of affordable products, services, or programs could we develop and launch to help thousands of people learn and do innovation step-by-step by working on their own projects?

More Specific Questions:

2. What kinds of digital products, services, or programs could we develop and offer?

3. What smaller offerings could help people learn about our more comprehensive programs?

4. What kinds of products could be offered on other platforms (like Amazon, iTunes, etc.) that already have a lot of visitors making purchases?

5. What kinds of offerings could we develop that integrate a lot of existing content already created?

Step 3:
Generate Ideas

Based on the previous two steps, you should have an innovation system to work with, a challenge to use, and some more specific questions to generate ideas on. You created these questions based on problems or opportunities related to your challenge, and you may have received validation or insight from your stakeholders through a survey or conversations.

One of the key fundamental purposes of the idea generating stage is to generate *a lot* of ideas. The more ideas, the more we have to work with for developing concepts.

Ideas are like raw materials. We want a lot of raw materials to build from. Plus, there is the chance that we may hit a home run and generate a good idea in the first stage. If a baseball player steps up to the plate 200 times, they will have a better chance of hitting a home run than if they only step to the plate 10 times. Their swing will probably get better after those first 10 times at bat, and so will your ideas.

One takeaway from this stage is that more ideas are better. For many of our projects where we develop new products, we may create a thousand ideas or more. For your project, fifty is a reasonable goal.

So, how do you come up with such a large number of ideas so you can develop a strong concept? First of all, you do it deliberately and purposefully. If you expect a bunch of brilliant ideas to come to you by chance, you are not going to get very far. You have to set out to intentionally generate these ideas. Schedule time to do it. Plan to do it. Schedule a brainstorm or innovation session, invite your collaborators, and execute.

You started by identifying a general category or space for your innovation by selecting a challenge that hopefully you are passionate about, value, and have knowledge or experience in. You came up with many specific problems or opportunities related to that challenge. You then turned those challenge problems and opportunities into questions. These steps make the idea generation easier, more focused, and more likely to develop a successful concept.

For instance, on a project we did online, we worked on the "environment" category from Google's project, and then brainstormed solutions to the plastic bag problem as a question to dig deeper.

You can view an example of this plastic bag brainstorm at:

brainreactions.net/brainstorms/1815

This example includes a question stimulated from a problem, hundreds of generated ideas, collaborative ideas from multiple people, selection and voting on good ideas, and sorting of the most popular ideas. This simple process is valuable for creating better and more innovative ideas.

What you get to do now is the fun part: idea generating. Focus on your question, and list, without judgment, as many ideas as you can. Ask others to collaborate with you as well. Focus on the two key rules of brainstorming:

1. Generate as many ideas as possible.
2. Do not judge your ideas!

So why is it so important to have a process that yields a lot of ideas instead of one idea that you just get by chance? Generating many ideas is a process-oriented feature of very effective innovation systems demonstrated in a lot of successful organizations. When they develop new products, they get many, many ideas in the pipeline. From there, they qualify the ideas and whittle them down into a handful of concepts. After that, they test the concepts while developing them more. In the end, they may only end up with a single new product from hundreds of product ideas.

This is how ideation for innovation works. More importantly, when you come up with a large number of ideas, it will be easier to do a more thorough analysis. You can identify themes that your ideas share.

Some ideas will lead to new and different ideas.

You will learn a lot from looking at all of the ideas you generate. You will see the forest from the trees. An innovation process is necessary to develop a better big idea.

Action 3: Look at your questions, and start generating a large number of ideas without judgment. Try to list at least 10 ideas right now.

Brainstorm with a group, or come up with a list of ideas for your question on your own. Make sure to number your ideas. This will help you get a higher quantity and organize them in the later stages of the innovation process.

Darin's Challenge Example:

Based on the challenge questions I created, I'm numbering and listing these ideas. I'm going for a large quantity quickly, and I'm not judging the ideas because I know that this is the idea generation stage, not idea analysis!

1. "Intro to Innovation" webinar
2. Online workshop program on step-by-step innovation
3. Live Google + Hangout walking participants through an innovation project
4. Binder of innovation tools and activities for facilitators
5. Amazon eBook on step-by-step innovation for your challenge

6. Membership site with many different innovation resources
7. Blog post series on innovation topics
8. YouTube video series featuring different innovation stages
9. Innovation podcast
10. Traditional-sized book published through CreateSpace
11. Q&A program where I respond by email, blog, or video
12. Innovation assessment surveys
13. "How To Innovate" guide as PDF on Smashwords
14. iPhone or Android app that guides users through the innovation process
15. Workbook of worksheets you fill in for your project
16. Idea list PDF of innovation techniques to use for any challenge
17. "Song" on iTunes that talks them through the innovation process
18. "Guided meditation" mp3 that helps you with innovation activities
19. Slideshare presentation on getting started with innovation
20. PDF of PowerPoint slide visual telling an innovation story that teaches the system
21. Online course about innovation

Step 4: Analyze & Synthesize Ideas

An increasing emphasis on the need to innovate is leading organizations and individuals to collect more ideas to fuel their innovation pipeline.

The increase in brainstorming sessions, idea submissions, and contests to fuel ideas for innovation is leaving individuals with significant lists of ideas. Many wonder where to start and what to do next with their idea lists. This calls for a story and a metaphor!

The Grey Ball

When I was in elementary school, my class took a trip to a small state park in Forestville, Minnesota. When you hear the name Forestville, it is natural to expect to go into a forest, so that is exactly what this group of 30 youngsters did. I remember the park ranger telling the kids that he would give a quarter to the first one that could find a grey ball in the forest. This was strange to us. We had never heard of such a thing, but we were up for the challenge. A quarter was a quarter, and they had hard stick candy for only 10 cents at the old Forestville country store.

As luck would have it, I was the first to find a grey ball. I gave it to the ranger, and he gave me the quarter. He then told us something amazing. He held up the grey ball in the woods and told us that it was once a mouse. I quickly looked at my hand with disgust. He then said that an owl will catch a mouse and eat the whole thing. The owl will digest all of the parts of the mouse that it needs, and spit out what it doesn't need. This grey ball of fur and bones is called an owl pellet. Fascinating.

As an adult, I traveled to San Diego to attend a conference for innovation professionals from a wide variety of corporations. One thing that stood out to me was that these professionals and their organizations had large amounts of ideas, but they lacked a way to quickly screen these ideas. During my presentation, I told the story of the owl, and I suggest doing what the owl does to the mouse.

Why not quickly take all of the ideas in, and then only keep and devote energy to digesting those ideas that you need, are beneficial to you, and belong in you. These are the ideas that match your criteria and address the challenge you decided to work toward in the early stages. Everything else can be spat back out in a grey ball of fur and bones.

In my world of ideation, more is better. The nice thing about ideas is that they are short and can be quickly read and judged. I regularly review, analyze, and synthesize lists of over 100 ideas and make quick decisions on them. The first stage is an important one - your quick review and selection of ideas. Many ideas just get read over because they already exist, are way too far out, or are not aligned with what the organization is about. But there are a fair amount of ideas that get digested and developed from this long list.

The key is to not get intimidated by the quantity of ideas, and to be process focused. *Process focused* means understanding that generating a lot of ideas is key to discovering something new or creating something innovative. The next step is to consolidate all those ideas, and start spitting out some grey balls! It is also beneficial to have at least a couple of owls analyzing ideas. What you digest may be different than what someone else digests, and you may be spitting out something healthy.

Action 4: Review your idea list like an owl, and highlight the good ideas. These are ideas that you feel passionate about and want to work on further. They may fit well with why you want to innovate and your challenge. While you are reviewing your idea list, take note of themes that you see. What do multiple ideas have in common? Synthesize. Write down and describe these themes.

Darin's Challenge Example:

Analysis of Ideas

Thinking about my original challenge and what was important - affordable, easy, wide reaching, etc. - I selected these ideas from my analysis.

1. "Intro to Innovation" webinar
2. Online workshop program on step-by-step innovation
3. Live Google + Hangout walking through an innovation project
4. "Binder" of innovation tools & activities for facilitators
5. *Amazon eBook on step-by-step innovation for your challenge*
6. *Membership site with many different innovation resources*
7. *Subscriber only blog post series on innovation topics*
8. YouTube video series featuring different innovation stages
9. *Innovation podcast breaking down each step of the innovation system*

10. Traditional published book
11. Q&A program where I respond by email, blog, or video
12. Innovation assessment surveys
13. *How To Innovate PDF Guide of Tips on Smashwords*
14. iPhone or Android app that guides through the innovation steps
15. *Workbook of worksheets you fill in for your project*
16. Idea list PDF of innovation techniques to use for any challenge
17. "Song" on Itunes that talks them through the innovation process
18. *"Guided meditation" style mp3 that helps you with innovation activities*
19. Slideshare presentation on getting started with innovation
20. *PDF of PPT slide visual telling an innovation story teaching the system*
21. Online course about innovation

Synthesis of Ideas

This was done while reading the idea list for analysis. I wrote down each theme into about a sentence in length. You can write each theme on a post it note if you like.

- "How To" style products in PDF format that guide a person step-by-step through innovation on their own challenge by showing examples.

- A system that serves as a guide, moving people along the steps through software or slide advancement.

- Leverage new teaching/collaboration technology for an online class that is a deeper dive into innovation.

- Focus on the user creating their own project through worksheets, activities, tools to apply immediately, etc.

- Digital educational products that are offered, purchased or used largely on someone else's site (like YouTube, Amazon, Smashwords, iTunes, etc.)

Step 5: Develop Concepts

Develop Concepts

When evaluating, analyzing, and synthesizing ideas, it is good to select ideas with specific criteria in mind. After your first stage of analysis, where you select the good ideas from the rest, you will need to be more selective in distinguishing the great from the good. These great ideas are the ones that you will devote more energy to conceptualizing.

Selecting and using criteria will help you to develop concepts that have a better chance of success, because they are grounded in what you want to accomplish and how you want to accomplish it. Google's Project 10^100 has suggested five criteria:

1. **Reach:** How many people would this idea affect?
2. **Depth:** How deeply are people impacted? How urgent is the need?
3. **Attainability:** Can this idea be implemented within a year or two?
4. **Efficiency:** How simple and cost-effective is your idea?
5. **Longevity:** How long will the idea's impact last?

You can create criteria specific to your challenge, too. Select your top ideas to conceptualize from your analysis and synthesis of your list based on not only your passion for that idea, but how well it fits with these criteria. If it fits some of your criteria - or using the Google example, has reach, depth, attainability, efficiency, and longevity - then it is a tremendous idea! The criteria will also help you compare ideas to determine which ideas to develop further.

The Google Project 10^100 process asks you to conceptualize your idea by answering a few questions. You can do this for some of your best ideas. Many of these questions are deserving of their own brainstorm to converge on the best ideas or answers.

- What one sentence best describes your

idea?

- Describe your idea in more depth.
- What problem or issue does your idea address?
- If your idea were to become a reality, who would benefit the most and how?
- What are the initial steps required to get this idea off the ground?
- Describe the optimal outcome should your idea be selected and successfully implemented. How would you measure it?

Action 5: From your analysis, produce three concepts that are more fully developed versions of the original ideas. Write a few sentences about each concept to explain it more fully.

Darin's Challenge Example:

eBook. A how-to guide teaching "Step-By-Step Innovation for Your Own Challenge" that can be distributed on Amazon for Kindle and Smashwords for other sites and formats. I could also offer this on my own website and in conjunction with live events. The eBook will guide readers through the innovation system, helping them learn and do by seeing a real example and doing activities.

Audio Files. An mp3 innovation guide that talks you through a specific innovation activity to do that could be valuable for almost any challenge. It could be a visualization, an idea generation tool, or a technique to communicate your new concept. Distribute through iTunes and sell like individual music tracks.

Membership Site. Member-only portal for subscription-based content on my website. I share real innovation stories and examples I'm working on so others can follow along to learn and do for their own project. Members can participate in a special Q&A session with me or leave comments on the site. I integrate other content I've already created in the form of blog posts, videos, activity sheets, etc. in the members only area.

Step 6: Test & Select Concepts

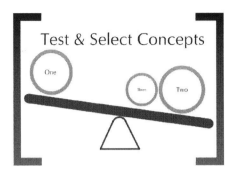

The whole purpose of going step-by-step through the innovation system is to launch something! Take action and bring a concept to life! I want to design a concept that is new and will have a positive impact.

It is essential to validate our concepts. You can do this yourself by using criteria that matter to you. Many times, these criteria are embedded in your challenge statement, or you may use general criteria like you will see in my example below.

You don't want to find yourself in a scenario where you spend a lot of time building an idea only for it to go nowhere. Believe me, I've done that plenty of times. I find it valuable to really test the concepts I develop against pre-defined criteria to make sure they have real promise.

It is also helpful to compare and contrast the top concepts you developed. This will help you know which one to develop further and launch.

The best way to move into action is to focus on a single concept to launch. Even though I may have a portfolio of top concepts and other ideas that I will further develop in the future, right now I want to focus on just one concept to develop further and launch. I also want to pick the concept that will have the best chance of being successful and be worthy of my time and resources.

To determine which specific concept to launch, I need to test and select from all the concepts I've created. I simply compare and contrast the concepts to each other, using the criteria that I've established for my challenge. Here is how I did that.

I compare my concepts to the criteria I have decided matter most for this challenge. I give each a 1 to 5 rating, with 5 being the highest score. I add up the totals, and this gives me a clearer picture of the strengths and weaknesses of each concept. From that score, I select which concept I should focus on developing and launching.

Darin's Challenge Example:

Concept Rating	eBook	Audio Files	Members Site
Easy to develop	4	3	3
Affordable	5	4	2
Helps people do for own project	5	2	4
Passion	5	2	3
Connection to other services	3	2	5
Launch to a large audience	4	3	3
Total	*26*	*16*	*20*

2. Which of these book title ideas do you think are the best? You can select more than one if you like.   🌀 Create Chart ⬇ Download

		Response Percent	Response Count
Innovation Step-by-Step: How to Systematically Create & Develop Ideas for your Challenge		30.0%	6
Practical Innovation		35.0%	7
Innovation Basics		10.0%	2
Quick and Simple Innovation		0.0%	0
Quick and Simple Idea Development		10.0%	2
Portable Innovation Facilitator		5.0%	1
Innovate Yourself		15.0%	3
The Simple Innovation Guide		20.0%	4
How to Innovate Step-by-Step: A Simple Guide to Systematically Create & Develop Ideas for any Challenge		45.0%	9
Develop Ideas and Innovate		5.0%	1
Other thoughts or comments on the title? Are there some better title combos perhaps? Show Responses			11
		answered question	20

Tool Tip: Another great tool at this stage (and almost every stage) is an online survey to your network or target audience. This can help you test and select as well as validate your concepts. I use surveys to let others help me make decisions and figure out how to communicate my concept. Any time you need to choose between multiple potential options, consider creating and sharing a quick survey with your stakeholders and colleagues. In the example above, 20 people helped me to select (and develop) a title for this book! You can see this book title survey at:

surveymonkey.com/s/PJTFWWM

Step 7: Communicate & Advance

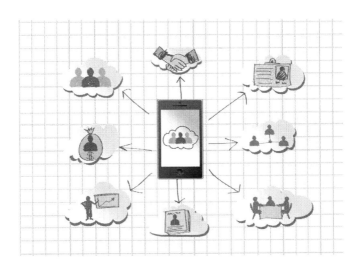

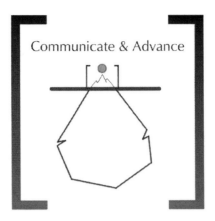

Communicate & Advance

You should now have a concept that is almost ready to be communicated to others. Is there anything else you can add to it to make it a stronger concept? You need to do more than just develop a great concept. You need to refine it.

What is often missing for success is being able to communicate your concept so that it is understandable, valuable, and memorable. Communicating your idea helps you take action on the concept, and gain buy-in internally and externally.

The Cone of Learning

Everybody learns differently, but presenting visuals is often a great way to engage people and make your presentation more memorable. I love this Cone of Learning visual from Edgar Dale. I understand and remember it better because it is an image I see instead of just text to read. People will learn more if you don't just let them read or hear, but also see.

How can *you* tell your story and show people your innovations?

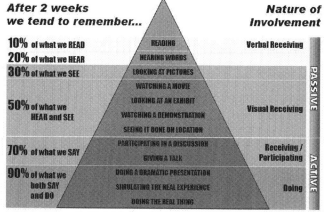

Cone of Learning (Edgar Dale)

After 2 weeks we tend to remember...		Nature of Involvement
10% of what we READ	READING	Verbal Receiving
20% of what we HEAR	HEARING WORDS	
30% of what we SEE	LOOKING AT PICTURES	
	WATCHING A MOVIE	
50% of what we HEAR and SEE	LOOKING AT AN EXHIBIT	Visual Receiving
	WATCHING A DEMONSTRATION	
	SEEING IT DONE ON LOCATION	
70% of what we SAY	PARTICIPATING IN A DISCUSSION	Receiving / Participating
	GIVING A TALK	
90% of what we both SAY and DO	DOING A DRAMATIC PRESENTATION	Doing
	SIMULATING THE REAL EXPERIENCE	
	DOING THE REAL THING	

Edgar Dale, Audio-Visual Methods in Technology, Holt, Rinehart and Winston.

We have a video program called Program Innovation where we teach people systematic idea generation and concept development by guiding them along the stages of this innovation system. We help people hear, see, and do. Most of us are communicating our creations on the web.

Instead of just text, why not try letting others hear

and see? It is easier than ever to create your own videos to do just this. Even a short, rapidly-created video will increase the potency of your communication over written words.

Instead of a paragraph of text about the innovation program, I will use one of the communication innovation tools and let you hear and see! Visit ProgramInnovation.com and take a look at what even amateur video producers can create with basic software and web tools like Prezi, Keynote, Power Point or screen capture software.

Use this as an example for how to communicate your own concept. How can you make it visual and help others to see, hear, and engage with the concept you created? How can they be a part of it, understand it, and take part in advancing it?

Share your innovation vision

Now that you have an innovation vision, share it with your colleagues. Get them on board. Have conversations with other people to get their suggestions and opinions. It is important to involve other people, including your stakeholders, colleagues, and students.

Activity 6: Create a message and plan to communicate your concept in an involving way. Create a visual or video about it.

Darin's Challenge Example:

This is the first version of the concept sheet I developed. I used this sheet to communicate my project to my colleagues and stakeholders.

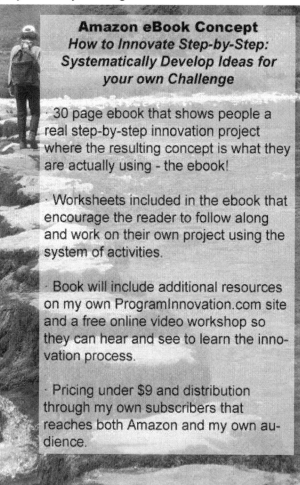

Amazon eBook Concept
How to Innovate Step-by-Step:
Systematically Develop Ideas for
your own Challenge

· 30 page ebook that shows people a real step-by-step innovation project where the resulting concept is what they are actually using - the ebook!

· Worksheets included in the ebook that encourage the reader to follow along and work on their own project using the system of activities.

· Book will include additional resources on my own ProgramInnovation.com site and a free online video workshop so they can hear and see to learn the innovation process.

· Pricing under $9 and distribution through my own subscribers that reaches both Amazon and my own audience.

Sustain Collaborative Innovation

You always need to be innovating. In our original challenge, we zeroed in on developing a new product - this innovation book. Ever since the development of the concept sheet about the book that we communicated and advanced, the product concept is still changing. Now, we have a new challenge: How do we launch and market the eBook? There is always a challenge to work on, and some challenges are logical next steps.

Innovation is best done collaboratively. We always want to engage our target audience, colleagues, customers, and experts in innovating with us. For example, I'm going to give my colleague, John, this eBook and ask for 15 minutes of his time to help me develop ideas for my new challenge. I'll have him contribute ideas and analysis for this challenge at each stage of the innovation system.

We can work together in a face-to-face meeting writing notes on paper, or we could meet electronically via Skype or Google video chat. If we want to collaborate online or from a distance, we can use Google Drive, in a spreadsheet or document. We can both see the progress on Google Drive, collaborating in real time.

Here, I have already clarified the challenge for John. Now that I have clarified the challenge and added some questions, I've asked John to contribute to my innovation process. I want to know what John's ideas are and which top concept he would want to move forward with.

Knowing that there are a lot of concepts that we will take action on at this stage in the process, this is a good opportunity for me to get validation for my ideas, get input on which ideas to forego, and hopefully learn some new concepts I hadn't thought about. In the end, I will use many of these ideas - my own, as well as ideas from John and other collaborators - to help me take action on my challenge.

Here's what I sent John:

Hi John,

Here's the challenge I was telling you about. Once you've read through the self-innovation eBook, I'd love to get your input. While you work through the process, please write your thoughts in the Google document I shared with you.

Thanks,
Darin

Challenge:
Marketing Communication and Outreach for

Innovation Step-by-Step eBook. How can we let people know about our new innovation eBook so they can learn about it, share it, or purchase it?

Questions:

- How can we market the eBook online utilizing social media and our social networks?
- How can we communicate the eBook on our own websites?
- How can we share the eBook within our live programs?
- How can we build a community around the eBook and engage the readers in co-creating?
- How can we promote reader engagement with others and us within the book?

Here's what John shared with me:

Hi Darin,

Thanks for sending your ideas along. I took some time to work through the eBook and included my thoughts below. I started with Step 2 since you've already clarified the challenge for me.

I've given you the first 20 ideas that came to

me, and I've highlighted my top 8 favorite ideas. I then synthesized those top 8 ideas into the three key concepts that I think we can act upon.

Once you've read through my notes, I'd love for you to bounce your thoughts back to me. Let me know if I can help with anything else!

Best wishes,
John

Questions:
- How can we market the eBook to different audiences effectively?
- How can we find the right people to market the eBook to?
- How can we use the eBook as a tool to convert readers to other programs?
- How can we develop a plan that markets the eBook at different times to different people?
- How can we get the eBook reviewed on blogs?
- How can we gather testimonials about the eBook's content?
- How can we differentiate this innovation guide from other eBooks like it?
- How can we incentivize sharing the eBook?
- How can we get people who learn about the

eBook to buy it?

Ideas:

1. *Offer group discounts or group packages for the eBook.*

2. Run A-B testing when marketing the eBook to our mailing lists.

3. Give discounts on other products and programs to people who purchase the eBook.

4. *Do multiple highly-targeted campaigns focused on specific uses of the process rather than one bulk, general mailing.*

5. *Make sure the eBook is available on all major eBook sellers.*

6. Create a free audiobook version of the eBook, available to anyone who purchases the eBook. (This means it can also show up as its own product, and it doubles the value of the product we're offering.)

7. Send preview copies of the eBook to innovation publication blogs.

8. Send preview copies of the eBook to blogs and people we have worked with in the past.

9. *Give the eBook away to everyone who has purchased a product, service, or program from us in the past. (These people can provide valuable testimonials and reviews on Amazon and other booksellers.)*

10. Give the eBook away at events. (These people could potentially become customers for other products in the future.)

11. *Include a survey in the eBook that can be filled out by people who go through the process. Use this survey to develop a second edition of the book, and give the second edition to owners of the first edition for free.*

12. Partner with blogs to provide articles about the eBook.

13. Cross promote the eBook at events and programs.

14. *Launch a free kick-off event at public innovation and co-working spaces to teach people about the innovation system.*

15. Run a contest that gives away prizes for the best and most creative uses of the process in the eBook.

16. *Make sure the eBook is part of Google Books, making the content searchable online.*

17. Look into publishing physical copies, giving people more options for how they would like to use the system.

18. Showcase examples on the blog and social media of people using the guide effectively and successfully.

19. *Use the innovation system again 1 week, 1 month, and 3 months after launch.*

20. Continue to create great content in order to

build on what we've created with this eBook.

Synthesis of Ideas:

Make the eBook as accessible as possible to as many people as possible.

Divide our audience into different cohorts and market accordingly. People are different, so make the content applicable to them as such!

Listen to our readers and collaborators to improve this product and others. Innovators never rest on their laurels!

Develop Concepts:

Group Discount Programs. We know that successful innovation requires collaboration, so we've made it clear to our readers that there is an incentive to getting this self-innovation guide into the hands of their stakeholders. We should make that easy by providing a discount to groups, with better discounts available to larger groups. We should also encourage people we have worked with in the past to get this eBook by offering it to them at a discount or for free. We could also keep the cost of the eBook low to begin with, so people don't have to question whether they are getting their money's worth.

Automated Free Member Updates. We can add value to this eBook by promising readers free updates to the content. Digital distribution allows us to improve the eBook at a very low cost, so we should take advantage of that. Using free tools online, we can create a survey and solicit responses from our readers. That will allow us to gather email addresses to send all future versions of the eBook for free. We can also run through this exact innovation process again at regular intervals to both improve the eBook and refocus our efforts to market it.

Wide Online Platform Distribution. This eBook needs to be everywhere! We can use platforms like Smashwords to make the eBook available in multiple marketplaces at once. We can also submit the eBook to Google Books, which will make the content searchable online. When someone searches for something that exists in the eBook, they will get a preview, as well as links to purchase the eBook.

Test & Select:

Here, I've used some of our example criteria to help select the top concept from the three that I've synthesized. Each concept has a rating for all criteria out of 5 possible points.

	Group Discount Programs	Free Member Updates	Wide Online Platform Sharing
Easy to develop	5	4	4
Affordable	4	3	4
Passion	3	5	5
Connect to other services	4	1	1
Launch to a larger audience	4	1	5
Total	20	14	19

Communicate & Advance:

Group Discount Programs.
Let's run a special discount program available to three different groups of people at launch. This will incentivize getting people using the innovation process right away. We'll run three highly-targeted campaigns to offer discounts to organizations,

businesses, and people who have been part of any of our programs in the past.

- *Group 1: Our Subscribers.* This is the group of all people we have worked with in the past. Specifically, we can target our subscribers who have attended events and programs that use the innovation system described in this eBook.
- *Group 2: Partnering Associations.* We can partner with associations such as the Center for Creative Leadership, the American Society for Quality, and the International Leadership Association. These associations can offer the eBook to their members at a discount since we already know they value innovation.
- *Group 3: Organizations.* This is the group of businesses and other organizations that can gain value by using the innovation system described in this eBook. By offering a discount to these groups, we give them an incentive to get their entire organization innovating together.

By offering these special discounts at the launch of this eBook, we get more people innovating faster. We also give them a great incentive to get interested in the eBook right away, rather than waiting. In addition to group discounts, we can price the eBook affordably from the very beginning, which will ensure that the eBook is accessible to people without a group in mind right away. Creating a discount code is something that could be set up.

Here is a screenshot example of a group discount offered by the Center for Creative Leadership. We could also use a simple code too.

Do it Again

Congratulations! You have hopefully started all of the activities in the innovation system. You have advanced through all of the steps we identified in this system and looked over my shoulder at examples from my own project and what Google recommends.

Your task now is to do it all again. Go through the steps for a new challenge. Sustain the innovation. Keep living this process. Always be developing and communicating ideas.

Innovative organizations are always innovating. They are always generating new ideas in response to emerging problems and opportunities. You can do the same thing. You are an innovator and that is what innovators do - innovate.

Worksheets

As a reader bonus, you can download our full-size PDF workbook, which includes these worksheets and our visual innovation journal at InnovationSteps.com/book.

Step 1: Clarify the Challenge

Identify your problems and opportunities to clarify a meaningful challenge you can work on. Get the opinion of customers, users, and colleagues. What do they think the problems and opportunities are? What is the real challenge you can begin to work on? Write out your specific challenge statement.

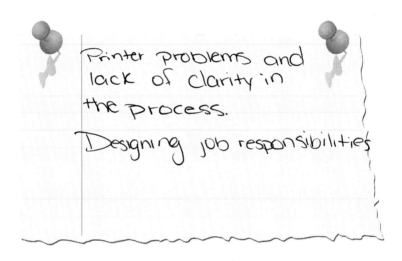

Printer problems and lack of clarity in the process.
Designing job responsibilities

Step 2: Formulate Questions

Break down your challenge. Turn that challenge into a series of more specific questions. Write down the most important questions to focus your challenge and be able to gather ideas.

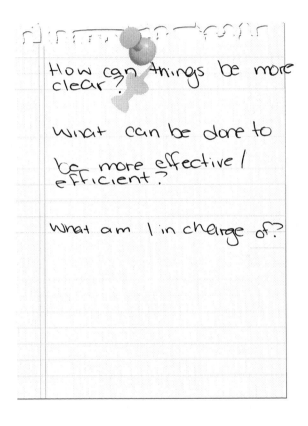

How can things be more clear?

What can be done to be more effective / efficient?

What am I in charge of?

Step 3: Generate Ideas

*Use your focused questions to spark ideas. Create many short
ideas. Generate them yourself, and gather them from outside
sources. Observe what ideas arise, but don't judge them yet!
Jot the ideas down on post-it notes. Go for quantity!*

Create folders for invoices
Look at new software
Ask more questions
Take more notes
Have a deeper
understanding of
tasks
Know where to look
for answers

Color code everything
Be more involved
Print less
Focus more, see more
Get a closer printer
Cross train roles

Know who to ask
Create a clear
manual
Talk to others
More examples
Create work patterns
Be super organized
Be more efficient

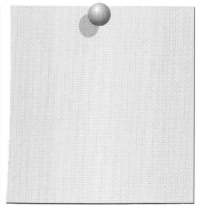

Create organized
work patterns
that define what
is expected where
it lists resources
and helpful information

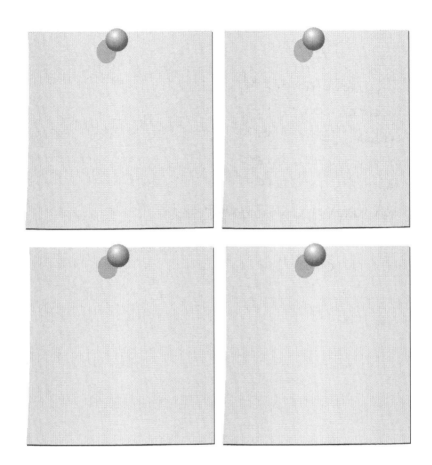

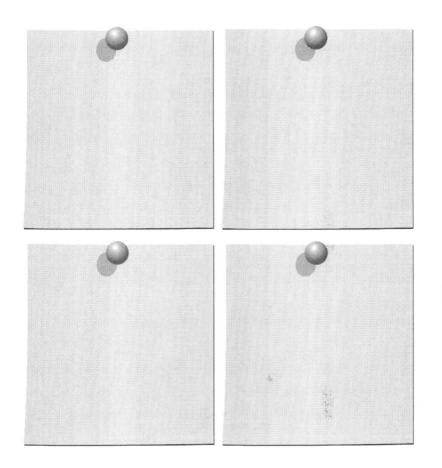

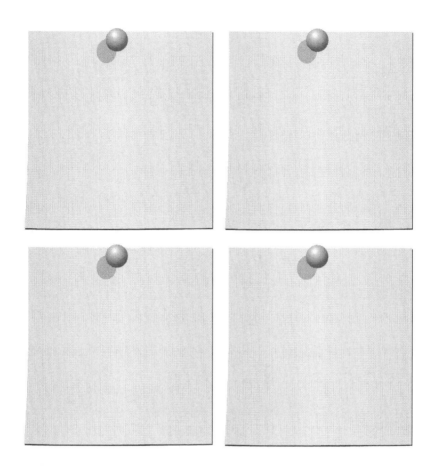

Step 4: Analyze & Synthesize Ideas

You have a lot of ideas; now quickly sort them out. Put them into a funnel to narrow them down. Highlight or write out in a bit more detail your best ideas...the ones you want to develop further. Also, see what themes naturally emerge in your idea list. Describe those themes as short statements.

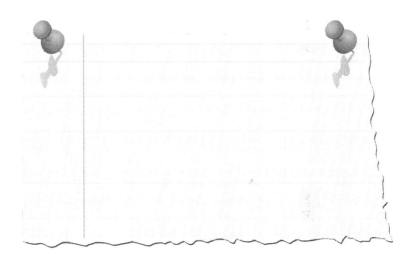

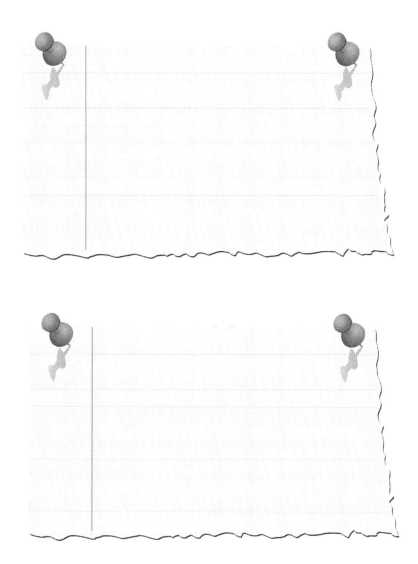

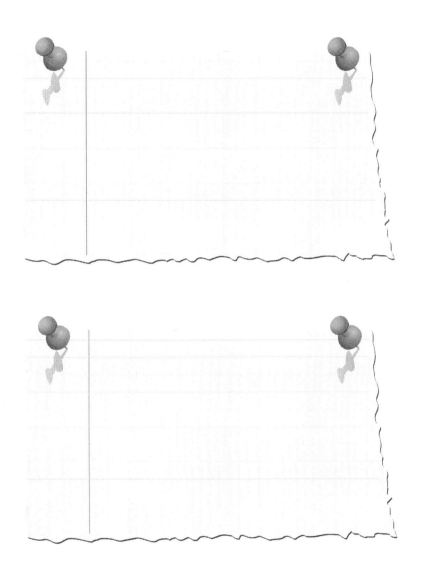

Step 5: Develop Concepts

Flesh out your ideas even more. Build and extend them. Add bullet points or more description. Develop the best ideas you narrowed down into full blown concepts. Write a few concepts out.

Step 6: Test & Select Concepts

Validate and test out the concepts that remain to see if some are better than others. Rate them and check with your stakeholders to see which concept is worth taking action on.

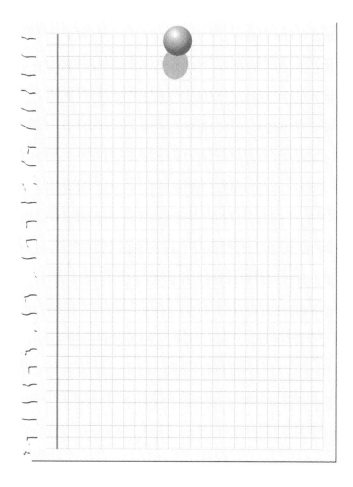

Step 7: Communicate & Advance

Communicate your top concept to gain feedback to improve it and your skill at communicating it. Create a slide, storyboard, or even YouTube video to explain it, and share the benefits. You went through the innovation system for the purpose of launching your idea. It can always be improved. Get into action sooner, rather than later. Now is the time to communicate and move forward!

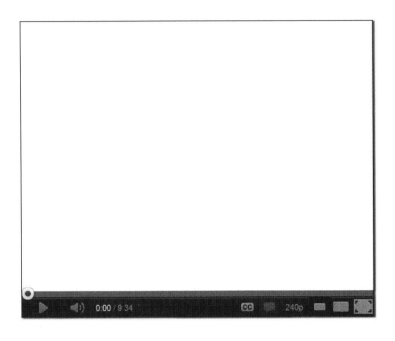

STEP 1

CLARIFY THE CHALLENGE

WHAT DO YOU WANT TO WORK ON?

1. IDENTIFY PROBLEMS
2. IDENTIFY OPPORTUNITIES
3. GATHER RESEARCH
4. CLARIFY A MEANINGFUL CHALLENGE

WRITE OUT A *specific* CHALLENGE

INNOVATIONTRAINING.ORG

114

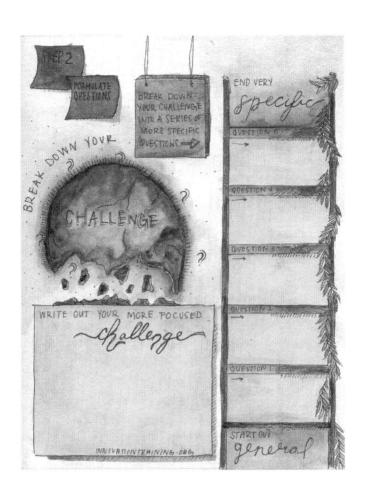

STEP 2

FORMULATE QUESTIONS

BREAK DOWN YOUR CHALLENGE INTO A SERIES OF MORE SPECIFIC QUESTIONS ➡

BREAK DOWN YOUR

CHALLENGE

WRITE OUT YOUR MORE FOCUSED *challenge*

INNOVATIONTRAINING.ORG

END VERY *specific*

QUESTION 5

QUESTION 4

QUESTION 3

QUESTION 2

QUESTION 1

START OUT *general*

STEP 4

ANALYZE AND SYNTHESIZE YOUR IDEAS

Throw your ideas into a funnel and narrow them DOWN

Highlight & expand on your best ideas

DESCRIBE NATURALLY OCCURING THEMES!

INNOVATIONTRAINING.ORG

117

STEP 5

DEVELOP CONCEPTS

what ideas can be combined?

Flesh out your ideas even more

Develop top ideas into full blown concepts

Add a header and bullet points for each concept

1.

2.

3.

WHAT IDEAS CAN YOU MASH TOGETHER?

STEP 6

INNOVATIONTRAINING.ORG

Test & Select Concepts

TEST & SELECT CONCEPTS

Rate your concepts and test them OUT!

	CONCEPT 1	CONCEPT 2	CONCEPT 3
Can I do this well?	◊◊◊◊◊	◊◊◊◊◊	◊◊◊◊◊
Do people want this?	◊◊◊◊◊	◊◊◊◊◊	◊◊◊◊◊
Is this concept profitably scalable?	◊◊◊◊◊	◊◊◊◊◊	◊◊◊◊◊
Have I bounced this idea off potential users?	◊◊◊◊◊	◊◊◊◊◊	◊◊◊◊◊
	◊◊◊◊◊	◊◊◊◊◊	◊◊◊◊◊
TOTAL SCORE			

119

Step 7

Communicate and Advance

COMMUNICATE / ADVANCE

What is your idea?

THE KEY TO A SUCCESSFUL CONCEPT IS COMMUNICATION

Detailed Description

Who is it for?

USE THE SPACE BELOW TO:
1. Collect Reliable Research
2. Begin to develop a Story
3. Sketch out prototypes

What problem does it solve?

What makes it different?

INNOVATIONTRAINING.ORG

About the Author

 Darin J. Eich, Ph.D. is founder of *InnovationLearning.org* and author of *Root Down & Branch Out: Best Practices for Leadership Development Programs*. He is a professional speaker, innovation facilitator, product & service creator, and program designer helping organizations like Dartmouth College, Procter & Gamble, the University of Wisconsin, USA TODAY, and the United Nations.

Darin lives in Madison, Wisconsin and is passionate about helping people to become more creative, innovative, and successful leaders. Learn more at *InnovationTraining.org*.

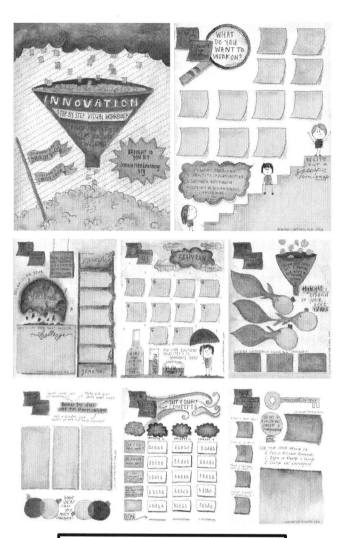

Find premium content and innovation resources at

InnovationSteps.com/book